WHICH FATHER

are you *following?*

By Robert Palmer

ISBN 0-937580-11-2

WHICH FATHER ARE YOU FOLLOWING?

Set up and printed 1987

Life In Christ Ministries, Inc.
12892 Fillmore Street
Mishawaka, Indiana 46545

CONTENTS

FOREWORD

Evangelist Bob Palmer is a long-time personal friend of mine, and of the LeSEA Ministries. From among us he went away to Bible college and then into missionary evangelism.

This book will describe for you the ministry God has put within his heart. This book will reveal to you that Jesus Christ is the same yesterday, today and forever.

I rejoice for every victory in the Bob Palmer ministry, and believe that he has a strong future in the Lord Jesus Christ. I believe the contents of this book will be a blessing to those who read it.

Brother Palmer has made it very clear as to which father he is following.

1

What You See Is What You Get

Are you in need of a miracle? The God I know and the God I serve enables me to be fully persuaded that HE WANTS YOU TO HAVE THAT MIRACLE TODAY!!

How can I persuade you that it is God's will? I am going to use WORDS to persuade you that God is on your side.

Did you know that God's Word will cause you to see what is inside of you? Jesus said in John 8:32, *And ye shall know the truth, and the truth shall make you free.* However, it is knowing it on the inside that causes you to be free.

Jesus knew who He was. He said, *...I am the way, the truth, and the life: no man cometh unto the Father, but by me* (John 14:6). He did not say that He was ONE of the ways to the Father, but I AM—THE WAY, THE TRUTH, THE LIFE!!

Buddha claims he is *a way* to God, but it is not true. There is only *one way!* You must realize that what you hear is what you see, and what you see is what you do. John 14:6 will cause you to SEE the right light. There are many voices in the world and if you listen to them, unless it is God's voice, they will lead you into the wrong path—the path of darkness.

God has a voice

The prophet Zechariah had a message from the Lord which he describes in Zechariah 4. *And the angel that talked with me came again, and waked me, as a man that is wakened out of his sleep, and said unto me, What seest thou?....*

The angel's message to Zechariah was, *...This is the Word of the Lord unto Zerubbabel, saying, Not by might, nor by power, but by my Spirit, saith the LORD of hosts. Who are thou, O great mountain? before Zerubbabel thou shalt* *become a plain; and he shall bring forth the headstone thereof with shoutings, crying, Grace, grace unto it.*

The Spirit of the Lord has the same message for the Church today. He has sent forth His angel who is awakening the Church out of its sleep. The angel is saying, "Church, what do you see? What are you looking at? Are you seeing God's Kingdom at work for you?" As He is shaking the Church, He is saying, "WAKE—UP—OUT—OF—THAT SLEEP. WAKE UP—AND—BEGIN—SEEING—WHAT I—HAVE—SHOWN YOU—THROUGH MY WORD!!" The Word will cause you to see!

Most believers think they have the right light. They say, "I'm a born-again Christian, and I'm walking in the fullness of God's Word." Are you? Jesus said in Luke 11:35, *Take heed that the light which is in thee be not darkness.*

The Lord has urged me to preach this message around the world. I challenge you, "Are you seeing A L L that God has for you?" Or are you in a little box saying, "I've got it all!"

What are you looking at? Are you seeing God's Kingdom at work for you?

The Box Mentality

Be careful that you do not place yourself in a little box and think that you have it all. The box will close up on you and while you believe you have it all, God is moving on with the rest of the Body of Christ. That is what has happened down through the ages in different denominations.

In Scotland and England, there are many beautiful big church buildings in which you may come and worship the Lord. Two hundred years ago they had the Truth and the power of God was working in their midst. Then man with all his intellect began to doubt. "Oh, I don't know if I can really believe this or not! Jesus was born of a virgin? God would not do it that way—He would choose a different way than that!"

Men, with all their intellect began watering down the Word of God, "The Lord could not do it that way." But the Word has not changed. From the very beginning God said, "My Word will never change!"

You must let this Word work on the inside of your heart. The entrance of this Word brings L I G H T! You do not have to be an intellectual to understand the Word. In fact, some people get so smart that they are going to hell smart. All you have to do to be able to see the Kingdom of God is to be born again. Then God's Word will cause you to see A L L the blessings He has for you.

The Visit In The Night

A Pharisee named Nicodemus, who was a ruler of the Jews came to Jesus by night. He said in John, chapter 3, "Rabbi, we know that you are a teacher come from God: for no man can do these miracles that you do, except God be with him."

Jesus answered him, "Except a man be born again, he cannot see the kingdom of God. That which is born of the flesh is flesh; and that which is born of the Spirit is spirit."

Nicodemus was an intellectual man, but he could not with his finite mind understand that you could not see or understand this kind of kingdom unless you were born again.

However, when God's Word comes into your heart—that incorruptible Word—you will be born again! Old things will pass away, and all things will become new. (II Corinthians 5:17). You will become that new creature in Christ Jesus! Then you will be able to see into the Kingdom of God, and see all that God has for you!

John 8:31 reads, ...*If ye continue in my word, then are ye my disciples indeed.* It is important to know that you must continue in His Word to be His disciples; it is being a disciplined person, putting the flesh under; it is letting God arise in your life, and c o n t i n u a l l y letting God's Word work on the inside of you. The entrance of His Word into your heart causes the Light to come on. It is not the entrance of this word into your head, it is the entrance of His Word into your h e a r t! That is what causes you to see a l l that God has for you.

How do you get light on a subject?

If you wish to have all the light there is on healing, you should look up all the scriptures there are on that subject and begin meditating on them day and night. Then you will be able to see and understand on the inside with the spirit man. It will cause the medicine of that word to shine on the inside of your heart.

He says, *The spirit of man is the candle of the LORD, searching all the inward parts of the belly* (Proverbs 20:27). Have you had your candle lit up? If not, you cannot see all that God has for you!

You must have your inward man lit up on

the inside to see God's Kingdom working for you. What are you meditating on? You are hearing words, but are you hearing the right words? If you are hearing the wrong words, that is what you are going to follow! As a man hears words, that is what he is going to see and what he is going to believe. WHAT YOU HEAR IS WHAT YOU SEE AND WHAT YOU SEE IS WHAT YOU DO!

There are M A N Y voices in the world and these voices are traveling all over by a spirit. By a spirit these voices come to your mind and you begin to meditate on what the ugly voices are saying and you become a product of these voices.

Deuteronomy 28 says that if you will listen to God's voice and obey His commandments, *Blessed shalt thou be when thou comest in, and blessed shalt thou be when thou goest out.* Observe what the Word says and become persuaded on the inside through these words so that they can cause you to see. You will be saying, "Oh, it just dawned on me... Oh, now I see!" The Word will become Light to you and you will walk in that Light; and it will cause you to become a DOER of the Word. It will cause you to walk in the miraculous. It will cause you to walk in the blessings of God—blessings already paid for!

Are You Waiting For God?

Are you waiting for God to do something? It is A L R E A D Y DONE! Now, you must receive it by faith.

Faith is what you believe in—and what you believe in is what you hear—and what you are seeing on the inside.

But are we not supposed to walk by sight? That is right, unless it is sight on the inner man. Without this sight you will not please God for this sight on the inside of you is your faith in God through His Word. What you HEAR is what you SEE, and what you see is what you are going to be a DOER of.

Everyone believes in something. You either believe that God heals or that God does not heal. Jesus warned you to be sure that your light is not darkness. You can believe a lie and be damned. You can believe a lie and walk in poverty—but you do not have to continue walking in poverty. Let me show you some wonderful truths.

Jesus became poor so that you might become rich!

Jesus became sin so that you might be made righteous!

Jesus became sick taking our sickness upon His body, so that you might walk in health!

Jesus left glory to bring you into glory!

In all these things *Jesus took your place.* All I have to do is persuade you to receive it and walk in it. It is that simple!

Watch Out—God's Gonna Get You

...Despisest thou the riches of his goodness and forbearance and longsuffering; not knowing that the goodness of God leadeth thee to repentance?
(Romans 2:4)

God is going to get you with His GOOD-NESS, because He loves you so much. Romans 2:4 says that His goodness will cause you to repent. "Repent" means to "turn around or to change your mind."

As God's children we must learn to think like God thinks. Philippians 4:8-9 reads, *Finally, brethren, whatsoever things are true, whatsoever things are honest, whatsoever things are just, whatsoever things are pure, whatsoever things are lovely, whatsoever things are of good report; if there be any virtue, and if there be any praise, think on these things.*

If God be for you, who can be against you!

God is on YOUR SIDE. Then who is against you? THE DEVIL!

The devil dislikes you intensely, not because of you, but because of Jesus. If he can stop you from believing on Jesus, he can stop God's plan. That's the whole story in a nutshell.

The devil wants to stop God's plan, but he cannot!

The last chapter of The Book declares that we win. God wants you to be a winner every day of your life.

The majority of the Church is asleep, but praise the Lord, I see the Church awakening and coming alive. In my travels around the world, I see revival fire. There is hope!

"What Seest Thou?"

The angel asked Zechariah, *What seest thou?* Now God is asking you, "What are you looking at?" If A L L you are looking at is your problem and your circumstances or your mountain—that is all you will have.

When you wake up in the morning do you say, "Good Lord, it's morning," or do you say, "Good morning, Lord"? Are you praying that you will make it to the end, or are you always rejoicing in the Lord?

The God I serve makes me an overcomer. I believe that God is on my side. He walks with me and I am convinced that He will never leave me or forsake me. The gates of hell are not going to prevail against me!

Did you know that the devil has had all of his teeth knocked out? All he can do is gum you! The Scripture says that he is going around *like* a roaring lion. It does not say he *is* a roaring lion, only that he sounds like one. Remember, the devil is a liar. He is the father of lies and there is no truth in him!!

Do not take your eyes off of God's goodness. Jonah 2:8 reads, *They that observe lying vanities forsake their own mercy.* When you begin to see all the lying vanities around you and get your eyes on them and not on God's goodness, then you forsake the mercy that belongs to you!

Speak To The Mountain

...This is the word of the LORD unto Zerub-babel, saying, Not by might, nor by power, but by my spirit, saith the LORD of hosts. Who art thou, O great mountain? before Zerubbabel thou shalt become a plain: and he shall bring forth

the headstone thereof with shoutings, crying,
Grace, grace unto it.

Zechariah 4:6-7

Who is the headstone the angel talked
about? It is Jesus! He is looking at the mountains that are before you and shouting,
"Grace, grace unto it."

Jesus is still shouting, G R A C E for grace
and truth came by Jesus Christ, but the law
came by Moses. Jesus came to bring grace
into your life. Grace is the willingness of God
to show His ability and power in your behalf,
even though you do not deserve it. He was
willing to send His Son, JESUS, into your life
to work for you.

What can you see? What you see is important because when you begin letting these
words get on the inside of you, they will work
their way to the outside. If you are believing
lies, you are going to have that mountain or
that impossible circumstance. However, if you
believe the Truth, and you begin to see this
Truth on the inside of you—WHAT YOU
HEAR IS WHAT YOU SEE AND WHAT
YOU SEE IS WHAT YOU ARE GOING TO
DO. You will be an overcomer!

2

Navajo Indian Medicine Man

A granddaughter of an 86-year old medicine man had taken hold of the Truth and was interceeding for him. It might seem impossible to reach someone who had been into witchcraft all of his life, and although it is hard, the Spirit of God and His anointing can penetrate any wall. It will make any wall tumble when we say, "Oh mountain, be thou removed!"

The medicine man was coming to the end of his life—he was dying of cancer and his foot was being eaten away exposing the bone. He had tried using his own medicine, but it did not work. Then he went to the doctor hoping that he could help him. The doctor told him, "I can cut your leg off, but it's not going to stop it. The cancer is too far advanced. Amputating your leg will slow it down a little bit, but you are going to die."

"Oh no! You're not cutting my leg off!"

His granddaughter brought him to the meeting. He hobbled up to the front row on crutches and his leg was all bandaged up. He was sitting on the front row as if to say, "OK. Prove your God." His had failed him. I am glad I have the answer to life's problems. It is Jesus Christ! The world is starving, but we have the dinner bell for the lost!

I preached Jesus and at the close of my message I said, "Bring that man up here. 'What's the matter with you?' I asked him. God is going to heal you!" I did not know that the man was deaf also, but it really did not matter. "He that hath an ear," the Bible says, talking about your spiritual ears, "let him hear what the Spirit has to say." Oh mountain, be thou removed! Oh cancer, be thou removed!

I laid my hands on the old medicine man although that was not necessary. The laying on of hands is nothing more than a transference, a touch, a release of faith. Most people are flesh oriented—they want to be touched. However, there are more people healed by hearing the Word than by anything else. I meet them in the prayer line. They were sick when they came, but are healed before I have a chance to pray for them. "I just want to make sure," they say. "It's all gone, but please pray some more."

I laid hands on the witch doctor but I did not know all that was happening to him. He told me later that when I laid hands on him, electricity went all through him. It was the Spirit of God removing the mountain from his life. It was removing the curse from him and breaking the powers of darkness. He could have gotten it all at once, but like most people, he got it on the installment plan! He spoke in Navajo, "I've got it! I've got it! But pray for my ears that I can hear."

We prayed for his ears and his ears opened. When he unwrapped the bandage off his foot, he said, "It's healed!" The cancer had eaten away the flesh and exposed the bone. I am glad I don't go by what I see or hear, but what I see in the Word of God. That is where it counts. I knew the Word says, "The just shall walk by faith and not by sight." It is not talking about your physical eyesight, but your spiritual eyesight. You have

spiritual eyes to see with and I could see him
healed right there. "I'm healed! I'm healed!"
he said joyously. If I had been an unbeliever
I would have said, "Oh no you are not! I can
still see the bone sticking through there." To
prove it a little bit further, faith is not only
a fact, but faith is an act! You are going to
act on your faith. You will do what you could
not do before. If you could not walk, you
walk. If you could not hear, you hear. If you
could not see, you see. You say, "I see in
the name of Jesus!" You put legs on your
prayers and you begin doing! The old man
led everyone in a Jericho march all around
the tent. He lifted up his hands and started
walking and praising God. "Hallelujah, glory,
glory, glory," he shouted. Did we have a good
time dancing on the old campground and
shouting the victory that night.

The next night the ex-medicine man was
back again on the front row. He had no
crutch or bandages and he was wearing
shoes. This time he brought his wife with
him. She was blind, deaf, and in a wheelchair!
Before I began preaching I called the old man
forward and asked him to tell us what God
had done the previous night. "He put his
hands on me and began to sing and chant,"
he said in his Navajo dialect. That's what the

witch doctors normally do. I said, "Let me look at your foot." He took off his shoe and there was brand-new skin where there was none before! Baby skin! New life! God will put Life where the revelation of His Word comes and what is happening on the inside will manifest on the outside. Faith is the substance of those things you hope for!

The ex-witch doctor brought up his wife on the platform and said, "Do it to her."

"Just wait," I said, "I like to preach the Gospel first!"

I preached the Gospel and God did His part. *He sent his word, and healed them, and delivered them from their destructions* (Psalm 107:20). She got out of her wheelchair and began walking and each step she took was a miracle. The miracle-worker is Jesus! He is the King of kings and the Lord of lords. He is alive in me and He is alive in you! Don't let the devil tell you any different. I have faith and my faith is working for me more and more every day. I am fully persuaded, aren't you? Faith will work for you if your faith is in God! What you hear is what you believe in. Be sure the voice you hear is coming out of heaven and not your television set. Proverbs 4:23 warns us, *Keep thy heart with all diligence; for out of it are the issues of life.*

Protect it, put a garrison around your heart. If all you watch is Gunsmoke, that's all you are going to get! If that is what you meditate in day and night, that is all you are going to have. If you are meditating on Edge of Night or Search for Tomorrow, you will not be looking unto Jesus, the Author and Finisher of your faith. Your television does not have any faith finishing tools in it, unless you of course turn your television dial to Holy Ghost-filled preaching.

Whatever you meditate on day and night is what you will have so make sure that what you meditate on IS God's Word. Then you will be blessed. You will speak out words of Life and it will be faith. Isn't it good to have God on your side? You are a winner!

3

Overdose On The Word

Take an overdose of the Word of God and it will enable you to become more than a conqueror through Christ Jesus who strengthens you! The very power of God will rise up on the inside of you, and if you have a blind eye, it will cause the blind eye to see. The Word will cause deaf ears to open and the lame to walk in Jesus' name, because there is power in God's Word.

What are you seeing? If you believe a lie, you will be bound, but if you believe the Truth, you will be set free! It is the anointing of the Spirit of God on the Word that causes the Light to shine on the inside of you giving you the same ability that Jesus had while walking on this earth.

As I travel all over the world, I meet people who are bound up because they have listened to a lie. They heard lies, so they walk in the knowledge of the lies that they have inside of them.

In India exists a caste system that dictates the way of life you may live. People I met agreed that they must be born again. They hoped that they would be born into a rich family the next time, rather than a poor one as in this life.

The devil took the Truth and perverted it and twisted it around. That is the only way he can get you to follow him; through taking a little bit of the Word and twisting it. That is what he has done to the Indian people through reincarnation! Reincarnation is a twisted lie! Those people believe that they have to be born again, and that part is true, but it is being born again of the Spirit that will get you to heaven. You won't be born again out of one caste system into another caste system, nor will you come back as a snake, a fly, or a cow!

No, no! When you are born again of the Spirit, all of the old things pass away, and all things become new. You might have been poor before, but when you get born again, you are born into the Kingdom of God—and it is rich!! Where God's riches are—there is no sorrow. *The blessing of the LORD, it maketh rich, and he addeth no sorrow with it* (Proverbs 10:22). However, you must be *born* into this Kingdom, you do not get into this Kingdom just because your grandma was a Christian, or your mother or your father were Christians. No, you have to be born again through the incorruptible seed of the Word of God. Each and every one of us must make that quality decision to choose to follow the Light of the Word.

When we are born into this Kingdom, we can have all the inheritance that belongs to us through the Word of God. When Jesus shed His precious blood that cleanses us from all sin, His last word and testament came into effect. He now gives us as the children of the Kingdom the right to come boldly to the throne of Grace and obtain the mercy that belongs to us.

The people in India have believed lies and are bound, but I know that if I preach this Word, and keep on preaching it, the Word will put out the darkness. Darkness cannot put out light. They will see the Truth and the

Truth will set them free!

I Want It!
How Do I Get It?

Does God demand that I crawl up some mountain to gain salvation? Do I have to crawl on my knees for miles, or whip myself with some chain and draw blood? *Not by works of righteousness which we have done, but according to his mercy he saved us, by the washing of regeneration, and renewing of the Holy Ghost* (Titus 3:5).

NOT BY MIGHT, NOT BY POWER, BUT BY MY SPIRIT, SAITH THE LORD!

When you believe with your heart, and confess with your mouth, the very Spirit of God comes. He takes the blood from the Mercy Seat and cleanses you from all sin. You then receive the inheritance that allows you to go directly to the throne of Grace and obtain A L L that belongs to you.

John 3:16 reads, *For God so loved the world, that he gave his only begotten Son, that whosoever believeth in him should not perish, but have everlasting life.* It is yours, and all that pertains to life and godliness is through this Kingdom. All you have to do is open your heart, and begin seeing this Truth. Jesus said, *Verily, verily, I say unto you, Whosoever committeth sin is the servant of sin. And the servant abideth not in the house for ever; but the Son abideth forever. If the Son therefore shall make you free, ye shall be free indeed. I know that ye are Abraham's seed; but ye seek to kill me, because my word hath no place in you, **I speak that which I have seen with my Father: and ye do that which ye have seen with your father*** (John 8:34-38).

Those are strong words. Jesus spoke those things He saw the Father do—and so do you!

Which Father Are You Following?

That is what I am asking you. The answer is very important because you will speak those things you see your father do!

If you are following Father God, you will speak, and do, and say the things that He has said in His Word, because that is all you will see before you. His Word is abiding on the inside of you. You will only want to do those things that Father God has said. It will cause you to walk in victory from morning to night, and throughout the night. A L L you will see is God's plan for your life before you. You will have His Vision in front of you—it will be the world; it will be reaching out and touching lives; changing lives; and bringing LOVE into the world. There will be no room for hatred or bitterness—not in God's Kingdom! There is nothing but God's peace, and God's joy, and God's love to flow to you. The Word will be shining on the inside of you and you will not listen to the lies out there. The Father of Lies will try to speak to you, BUT you will not follow that voice. Jesus said, *My sheep hear my voice, and I know them, and they follow me* (John 10:27).

Jesus is talking to you, Church! But the devil wants to speak to you, too! His voice is running rampant throughout the earth and it is trying to get into the Church. It is up to you to say, "NO SATAN! GET THEE BEHIND ME!

Satan even came to Peter, and Jesus said, *Simon, Simon, behold Satan hath desired to have you, that he may sift you as wheat* (Luke 22:31). Satan wanted to use Peter. Once he even spoke right through Peter to Jesus. What did Jesus answer him? "I REBUKE YOU SATAN!" He spoke to the devil who was speaking through Peter.

WATCH OUT, CHURCH! Do not let the devil speak through your mouth!

Speak only those things that you hear from your Father. Let His Word alone shine on the inside of your heart and—SPEAK THE WORD ONLY. Your whole household will walk in TOTAL FREEDOM because you walk in freedom!

The Psalmist says, *Thy word is a lamp unto my feet, and a light unto my path* (Psalm 119:105). The Word (Jesus) will lead you, and He will guide you into a supernatural way of life. The power of God will flow in and through you and throughout your household, as you let nothing but this Word—not circumstances around you—dictate the words that you speak. Your mouth should speak the Word only; and nothing else! Your mouth should always have a good report and not an evil report! The Word says that the mouth of a righteous man is a well of life. That is you and me, Church! We are the righteousness of God in Christ Jesus and we must walk in this Truth daily and let God's Word flow in and through us!

I have observed areas where the Church really needs to have a repentant heart. Repentance needs to come to the Church as well as to the rest of the world. The Church needs to change its mind from thinking the way the world thinks to thinking the way God thinks!

Only when we think like God thinks will we
ever see the Glory of God revealed in our
midst.

4

The Blind Lady

The Kingdom Of God Within Her

I was in Kirkcaldy, Scotland, preaching the Gospel to a group of Bible students. In the evening we had a healing crusade and I was preaching about the Kingdom. My text was Matthew 6:10. *Thy Kingdom come. Thy will be done in earth, as it is in heaven.*

On the second row sat a lady who was blind in one eye and almost blind in the other. The eye glass for her good eye was so thick it looked like the bottom of a pop bottle. She was listening intently to my sermon.

I said, "There will be no blind eyes or deaf ears in heaven. There will be no cancer or poverty either. Furthermore, God said in Matthew 6:10 that we could have His will done in earth, just like it is up there. Get ahold of that truth. Don't let the devil steal that revelation from you."

All at once it became revelation to the blind lady's spirit. We call it faith. What you hear is what you see and what you see is what you are going to do. Keep seeing His Kingdom. Keep looking and seeking after it.

The blind lady got excited. She said to herself, "I don't have to have this blind eye anymore!" I was praying for people in the healing line when she tried to get my attention. She came up to me and said, "Brother Bob! Brother Bob!"

"Please get in the line, just like everybody else," I told her. "Wait your turn."

"But, Brother Bob," she interrupted, "my blind eye has opened up! I can see!"

"How could that be?" I said jokingly. "You didn't get in the prayer line."

"Well, Brother Bob, you told me I didn't have to," she replied.

I said, "I did?"

She replied, "Yes, you said just believe God!"

And when he was demanded of the Pharisees, when the kingdom of God should come, he answered them and said, The kingdom of God cometh not with observation: neither shall they say, Lo here! or, lo there! for, behold, the kingdom of God is within you (Luke 17:20-21).

The Word says it is according to your faith. Speak the Word only! When Jesus had spoken to the centurion in Matthew 8:10, He marvelled and said, *Verily I say unto you, I have not found so great faith, no, not in Israel.*

When the blind lady heard the Word, it became real to her. "Brother Bob," she said, "you told me the Kingdom has come and it is in me! I've got the Kingdom in me! *Thy kingdom come. Thy will be done, in earth as it is in heaven.* I see it. There are no blind eyes in heaven. I took my glasses off and told the devil, 'You're a liar!' Then I reached up and took ahold of my eyes and began to massage them, in Jesus' name. 'Eyes,' I said, 'I speak to you, eyes come alive in Jesus' name.' And it happened! I can see out of both of them. I don't need these pop bottle glasses. I can see!"

That is what faith is. Faith is speaking those things that be not as though they were.

She said, "I did not have it all at once, but it came gradually and by the time I got up to you I had it all!"

God is a good God. Stay on the winning side and seek His Kingdom. Look for Him— He is the Author and the Finisher of your Faith. He will cause you to grow in it. Keep pressing toward the mark of the high calling which is in Christ Jesus. Jesus is the one who will cause you to be a winner instead of a sinner.

The following year we returned to Kirkcaldy for another meeting and the ex-blind lady was there. She came running up to me. "Brother Bob, my faith is still working for me. I have a husband now." (*He that findeth a husband find a good thing.*)

I am urging you to seek His Kingdom and let His Light begin shining on the inside of you. It will cause you to come through that dark tunnel you are in where it looks like there is no hope. Keep looking toward the light. Psalm 119:105 says, *Thy word is a lamp unto my feet, and a light unto my path.* As you begin walking down that path, it will get brighter and brighter. Your future is as bright as God's promises! There is no darkness in the promises of God, it is all good! The Gospel is the power of God unto salvation unto him that believes. Only believe, He said, that's all. Have faith in God and trust Him.

Jesus wondered if He would find faith when He comes back to earth. I believe He will. It is getting stronger, faith is increasing. Revelation knowledge is being poured out throughout the whole earth. Wherever we go, there are people taking hold of this message and changing their world. Thank God for His Word!

5

Mountain, Be Thou Removed

When you get full of life and full of the Word, that is when you can speak to your mountain and say, "Who art thou O Great Mountain before me?" Knowing this Truth, out of the abundance of your heart your mouth will speak, "Mountain, be thou removed and cast into the sea!" You will not doubt, because your heart will be full of faith and full of the power of God. You will be filled with the Light because you are full of the Word of God. You will only speak the things that the Father has shown you, just like Jesus! He merely spoke the Words that He heard the Father speak— and so will you as He is your Father also.

I was in a church preaching and a young lady came into the meeting. She was born again and filled with the Holy Ghost that evening. She was very excited about her experience, but she wondered if there was any hope for her husband who was an alcoholic.

I asked her, "What have you heard the Word say tonight? Do you know that God's Word can cause that mountain of alcoholism to be removed? However, you have to be able to visualize it on the inside of you before it will happen. In other words, you have to become pregnant with this Word. You have to know that if God is for you, who can be against you? You have to believe this!"

She said, "Oh, I believe, I believe. I am fully persuaded already!" She was believing for her husband to get saved. Although a sinner can exercise his own will, we can pray and believe for his salvation. We can come against darkness and travail in prayer and intercession.

The young wife and I stood in the gap for her husband that night. We had no idea where he was or what he was doing, and if we had, we might not have prayed! He was outrunning the cops all over town, drunker than a hoot owl. He saw a box car on the railroad tracks and he quickly jumped in and hid in a corner. Did he get in a BOX! He could go no place! While he was in the box, he cried, "Oh, God, help me. Why did you get me in this mess, God?" It was his own fault, but he was blaming God. None of you have ever said that, have you?

At the very moment we were praying and interceding, he was crying out to the Lord for help. Finally, he quieted down and all at once he heard this voice, "Maybe you ought to be in church where your wife is!" That very day she had said to him, "We ought to go to church and get our lives straightened out. We ought to start serving the Lord!"

The young man had come to the end of his rope. He looked around at the mess and the box car where he was hiding. The Holy Spirit was ministering to him at the same time we were praying. The next night while I was preaching, he came running up to the front, crying, "I'm ready to get out of the box!" He committed his life to the Lord Jesus Christ that night. Believe me, there is nothing too hard for God, if you and I can only become fully persuaded on the inside of our hearts and we begin to see this Light shining on the inside. One way or another, you are believing something and it is either the Truth or a lie. You are either bound up in God's Word or you are bound up in lies and traditions of men.

The Christians in England and Scotland started out alright, but over the years the truth got watered down with the traditions of men. It reminds me of a water brook that is pure at the top of the mountain, but when it reaches the valley, it has become contaminated along the way by junk and sewage. But the Word will never change and it will work for you today. It still causes sickness to leave, it still opens blind eyes, it still opens deaf ears, and it will even cause the lame to walk. When you can see it on the inside of you, it will work for you! The entrance of this Word brings light and understanding and you become established in the Lord. When you read the Word you understand it one way or another; you are either growing wrong, or you are growing right; you are believing darkness, or you are believing Light. Jesus said in Luke 11:35, "Make sure your light is not darkness!"

Every day, I examine myself. When I hear someone say, "I've got it all," I know they don't have much! Don't be so dogmatic thinking you have it all, except when it comes to the blood of Jesus and the virgin birth.

Be dogmatic about that. Here is where it is
A L L at—THE WORD OF GOD!

Revelation Knowledge

We visited a town called Alnwick in
England. John Wesley visited Alnwick years
ago and said, "There is no hope for this
town!" John Wesley was a mighty man of
God. There were a lot of witch covens there
in that day and much darkness. In those days
they did not have the revelation knowledge
we have today. There has been an increase
in the knowledge of God and the light of
God's Gospel is being revealed to many
throughout this earth.

Three young ladies in Alnwick got ahold
of some video and audiotapes about the word
of faith and about intercession. They de-
cided to pray for the town that John Wesley
said there was no hope for. Intercession and
prayer will change things. God is *not willing
that any should perish, but that all should come
to repentance* (2 Peter 3:9). When they heard
that we were holding meetings in the area,
they drove two and a half hours to hear what
we had to say. After the service was over, they
told the man in charge of setting up our
meetings, "You've got to come to our town,
you've just got to. We know you are the ones

who are going to help break the bondage that is over our town."

We promised to come for one meeting. Truly there was no life in any of the area churches. The bishop over the whole area had denied the deity of Jesus Christ. He even denied the virgin birth on television. However, they were willing to let us use their church on a Friday night, since they were only using it for one hour each week anyhow.

Signs And Wonders

We had a Holy Ghost meeting! The people came by word of mouth and even a couple of elders of the church came to watch what was going on. The newspaper refused to advertise the meeting because they did not believe in advertising that God performs miracles and that God is love. If you wanted to advertise a witches' meeting, that would have been all right.

The people who came heard the uncompromised Word of God. I told them that everyone of them there believe in something. The question is, "What are you believing in, though? Are you believing the Truth, or are you believing a lie?

An atheist believes in something. He

believes there isn't any God. He is going to hell smart. Only a fool says there is no God.

When I gave an altar call, eight people received Christ as their Savior and fourteen were filled with the Holy Ghost. Then we prayed for the sick. Many deaf ears popped open. One woman who was both deaf and blind—she was in total darkness not being able to see or hear, however, she had ears to hear with on the inside. Jesus said in John 6:63, "...the words that I speak unto you, they are spirit, and they are life." The Holy Spirit is on these words, and the words cause life to flow!

I could tell there was something wrong with the woman's eyes, because she was wearing black sunglasses. As I was speaking the Word, I just knew that God was working on her. After the service, I layed hands on her ears, and God instantly opened her ears and she could hear. She took her glasses off and I spoke to her eyes, "In Jesus' name, I command you to see!" Just like that her eyes opened up, and the power of God was released in her. A little white-haired lady—totally set free!

Three people were set free from cancer that night. One woman had had cancer in her stomach and the next day she told everybody she met, "I'm healed! I'm healed! I just want you to know I'm healed!"

The woman who had been blind and deaf testified to everybody she met, "I'm healed! I can hear and I can see!!!" She went to her son six times and kept repeating, "Son, I'm healed! I can hear and I can see!!!"

"I believe you, Mom, I believe you. You told me six times!"

The LIGHT put out the darkness in that town. Darkness cannot put the Light out, if you don't permit it. But you must continue in the Word, it is a continuous thing! You cannot have the Doris Day doctrine, "Whatever will be, will be, the future's not ours to see"

The future IS yours to see! You can have whatever you SEE on the inside of you. When you let this Light SHINE on the inside of you, you can have that mountain in your life removed and cast into the sea. There will be no room for doubt on the inside of you. You will be able to shout out, "GRACE! GRACE!" Grace is the willingness of God to show His mercy on your behalf even though you do not deserve it. It is the love of God that was poured out on Calvary for you and me that makes it possible. He loves you so much!

Is He Kidding Us Or
Is This For Real?

We ministered on the Isle of Man off the west coast of England and God moved mightily. The churches on the isle were reluctant to receive us or our message so we ministered from house to house preaching this Word of Faith. The island is 30 miles long and 12 miles wide with a population of 60,000 people. There are 13 witches' covens and many spiritualist churches on this little strip of ground. Despite all of the demonic activity on this island there were still many hungry hearts ready for the Word of God.

During one of the home meetings, three ladies were saved who had never heard the Gospel message before. They had never heard that you could be born again. All three ladies had multiple schlerosis. None of them knew that God is still healing people today. As I was preaching, one of the ladies exclaimed,

"Are you joking with me? Are you kidding us here today?"

I said, "No, I'm not joking, I'm not playing games, I'm telling you the Truth. I'm telling you what the Bible says. God wants you healed and He wants you healed today!"

She looked at her friend who had the same disease and said, "Is he kidding us or is this for real? Is God really alive? Does God really want us healed?"

I continued to preach even with the interruptions and gave the call for salvation. All three ladies responded to the call and I prayed for each one to be healed. They all received their healing by faith and one received an instantaneous miracle and got up out of her wheelchair and walked. Praise God!

You're Spoiling Our Fun!

We scheduled an hour service on an open-air stage during a medieval fest in Alnwick, England. This city was very wicked and the festival was a celebration of sin. We hired a Christian band to play 45 minutes and then I was to preach for 15 minutes. As the singing group began to sing, the anointing of God went through the air dispelling the darkness and a wonderful peace settled over the crowd. The group sang a song, then the leader testified about how Jesus changed his life, and the group sang again. The leaders of the festival became more and more upset. Finally they told them to get off the stage. One of them shouted, "You're spoiling the fun we're having. Quit it!"

The singers said, "You promised us the whole hour up here and we have only been up here about 30 minutes. And you promised our friend that he could speak for 15 minutes."

They replied, "No! We're not going to let him get up there!"

It was as if they knew what I was going to say. We pleaded with the leaders of the festival to let me have just a few minutes. They finally agreed to let me have two minutes. I got up on the stage and said, "Lord, I call upon your anointing, right now!" Then I grabbed the microphone, I had no time to turn to the Bible, and began to speak.

"They have only given me two minutes, so I'm going to give you all that I can give you in two minutes. My text is Mark 16:15-17, *Go ye into all the world, and preach the gospel to every creature. He that believeth and is baptized shall be saved; but he that believeth not shall be damned. And these signs shall follow them that believe...* "Jesus told us to go into all the world and preach Good News. We've got Good News for you! We've got the News that Jesus loves you! We have John 3:16,

For God so loved the world..." I shared with them Hebrews 13:8, *Jesus Christ the same yesterday, and to-day, and for ever.* I said, "He is still healing sick bodies, He is still setting the captives free! God is still opening blind eyes, He is still opening deaf ears, and He is still making the lame to walk!"

At that moment the leader started yelling out, "Shut up! Shut up! Don't say anything more!" And he ran over and pulled the plug on the amplifier. He pulled the speakers, but he could not pull the plug on the Holy Ghost. The Spirit of the Lord kept moving on the people. Everyone in the crowd just stood there without saying a word. The Spirit of God was speaking to their hearts. The people recognized that darkness was trying to stop this Good News that they were hearing. The devil had overplayed his hand.

We went down into the crowd and began to witness and hand out flyers and tracts to the people. We told them about the miracle meetings we had scheduled in the town. The people were so hungry and asked many questions. God was moving in that place.

As I moved among the people, I shook hands with a man, and unbeknownst to me, the power of God shot through his hand.

He knew it had to be God when the electricity went through him. That evening, he and his family were gloriously saved in the miracle crusade. Many others received salvation, healing and deliverance. Glory to God, His Word is working. The church is waking up. Mountains of doubt and unbelief are being removed.

Denying God's Power

In Glasgow, Scotland, sixty churches closed their doors in 1985! They had "a form of godliness, but they denied the power thereof!" When you leave the Spirit of God out, God cannot move! The people in the sixty churches not only left the Spirit out, they left the Word out along with it. You cannot do that; the Spirit and the Word must work together. If you overdose on one, you will get out of balance one way or the other. You need to overdose on both, Spirit and Word! God's Word ALWAYS agrees with the Spirit.

6

The Maniac In The Cage

While we were ministering in the Philippine Islands, we heard of a man who was demon possessed. They had kept this poor man locked up in a cage for eleven years. A missionary friend of mine said to me, "Brother Bob, I have heard that you cast out devils in the name of Jesus."

"Sure enough," I replied, "I'm a believer!"

Then he told me, "Well, my wife and I went over to the island where this man has been locked in a cage for eleven years. We intended to cast the devil out of him. Mind you, he had not spoken a word in all that time, but when he saw us, he rose up and said, 'I know who you are. You're the Light!' ''

Isn't that interesting? The devil knows something, doesn't he. He will probably say that about you, too, and it is a good compliment. Then he said this, "But I don't want you!"

Of course, he didn't. It forces him out of the house that he has occupied.

So my friend said, "Well, guess we can't do anything!" And they left, but continued to pray and intercede for this man and even sent Bible school students to pray for him also.

I promised my friend that I would go. It was difficult to get there as we had to take a boat for several hours to reach the island and then walk to the center of the island where the demon possessed man was kept. What a sight! The cage was filthy since nobody had ever bothered to clean it out. The man inside was just skin and bones. I was wondering what to do when all of a sudden I heard a voice saying, "Go in the cage!"

Now remember, if you are led by the head, you are dead. So I asked, "Who's got the key?"

When they finally located the key and unlocked the door, my friend said, "Do you want me to lock it up behind you?"

"You be led of the Spirit of God—I am!" I replied.

The demon-possessed man and I went slipping and sliding around the cage as I bound the Strong Man in that man and told the devil to come out of him. He spoke to me in perfect English, "No, I'm not coming out!"

"Oh, yes you are! Darkness, come out, in Jesus name!" I commanded with a strong voice.

I continued speaking to it, telling it to come out in Jesus name. I was holding his head and as I looked into his eyes, I saw *two* pairs of eyes, not one. (The eyes are the windows of your soul.) He was cursing and screaming, and I continued to tell it to come out through the precious blood of Jesus Christ that cleanses this man of all his sins. "You have to come out, devil!" I commanded again. About that time, he was loosed and tears started flowing down his face. He was not able to speak any more English and I had to have an interpreter to talk to him.

For eleven years he was bound by Satan!

Recently when I was in prayer, I all at once had a vision. In my vision I saw the man as he had been before his deliverance. I was told that this man would sit and stare at a corner hours at a time, sometimes all day. I saw a demon in that corner, telling him, "You ain't getting out of here. I've got you now and you ain't getting out of here!"

Even worse than being locked up in a cage was that he was bound up on the inside. The devil was telling him that he was going to keep him in the box. The devil will do that to you whether you see him or not. He will tell you, "You ain't getting out of here and there ain't no hope for you. You can't make it in this life!"

Maybe the devil has been telling you, "You are no good. You were born poor and you are going to stay poor." Or perhaps you have heard him say, "You're worthless. In fact, you are not worth anything!" He will speak ugly words to you that will keep you bound up in chains of darkness.

But I have good news for you! Jesus said, "The Spirit of the Lord is upon me. He has anointed me to preach this Gospel to...

•those that are bound up with chains of darkness

- the captives, so that they might be set free,
- those that have a broken heart,
- those that are blind,
- those who are poor.

Because you walk in liberty, this Gospel will make you MORE than a conqueror; not just a conqueror—but MORE THAN a conqueror! This Gospel will cause you to win. I know and am fully persuaded of it, because I was bound—BUT now I'm free!

7

Two Days To Live

I was dying of cancer, and I did not believe in Jesus. As a matter of fact, I did not want Jesus in my life. My father-in-law was a deacon in his church and he had tried to witness to me several times, but I did not want salvation—no, not me!

He came into the hospital to visit me one day. I had been given 52 Cobalt treatments, but they said there was no hope for me. They gave my wife the ugly report, and I was so negative I didn't care. "I am ready," I said, "let me go!"

But my father-in-law came into the hospital room and he spoke words. Words are powerful. Luke 5:15 says, ...*great multitudes came together to hear, and to be healed...* The

Psalmist says in Psalm 107:20, *He sent his word, and healed them, and delivered them from their destructions.*

Proverbs 4:22 says, *For they are life unto those that find them, and health to all their flesh.*

Matthew 8:16 says, ...*and he* (Jesus) *cast out the spirits with his word, and healed all that were sick.*

By His Word! My father-in-law spoke words that were full of life and which caused the darkness to flee. My first reaction was to laugh and mock him. I also had faith, but my faith was that I didn't believe, I didn't need it.

Just at that split second, and that is all it takes, I accepted those words!!!

The Word says that if we have faith the size of a mustard seed, that is all it takes. You only have to open your heart a little bit. "Bob," my father-in-law said, "Jesus loves you!" It pricked my heart and I opened up and in came the Light. It began shining and I began to weep and cry. Then the glory of God came upon us and he laid his hand on me. It was like honey out of heaven. That is the only way I can describe it—the very glory of God came shining on the inside of me and

I wept and I cried. I knew at that moment that GOD IS LOVE! It caused me to see differently—right then—and I did not know all there was to know about God. I had never been to church in my life.

The doctors prophesied to my dear wife Nancy and said, "In two days your husband will be dead." It was true! In two days I was dead. Old things passed away, and behold, all things became new! I am a new creature in Christ Jesus. It is no longer I who live, but Christ in me, the Hope of Glory!

They sent me home well in body, but I did not become a saint overnight. I had to grow up spiritually. My old mind needed to be washed out, and the Word of God did wash it clean and I was renewed.

The Word of God is so important. It will cause you to grow up spiritually and it will cause you to see the glory of God and His goodness! I know the pit that I had been in. I am fully persuaded that there is nothing impossible with God. You have to experience it the same way. You must be fully persuaded for yourself!

8

Choose You This Day...

God loves you and He wants His very best for you, but it is your choice. The woman, whom I told you about in an earlier chapter, was both blind and deaf, how then could she see or hear?

She did not see with her physical eyes or hear with her physical ears. She had a heart that heard from God! God knows your heart!

There was another woman in that same meeting who I knew was unsaved. I found out later that she was involved in the occult and professed to be a witch.

"Do you want to be saved!?" I asked her.

"No," she answered flatly.

"Well, we have a choice in the matter and it looks like you've made yours!" I told her. That woman had seen the glory of God in the meeting. She had seen the Lord pour out His Spirit and anointing with miracles. She had seen the demons cast out, and the captives set free. But it was her choice. She chose to walk out the same way she came in. God will not force you to be a Christian! He will not make you walk in all that He has for you. He says, "Choose you this day whom you will serve!"

Fully Persuaded

A woman came into a meeting we had in Kirkcaldy, Scotland. She heard the Gospel, and it changed her thinking. She had been paralyzed by a stroke for years and had to be carried into the meeting. She heard that God was doing miracles and it was new to her. She had been taught that God's healing power was a thing of the past, and she had been persuaded by the message she heard. Now she was hearing a different Gospel, a Gospel that told her that God loved her and that He was willing for her to walk in health.

Her friends brought her to the altar, but before I could pray for her, she exclaimed, "Don't push me over like the rest of them!"

I told her, "I didn't push them over. Just lift your hands and praise God!"

"I can't," she cried. "I can only lift one hand."

I told her, "Lift the other one too."

"Oh! oh! oh!" she cried, "I did it!" The next thing she knew she found herself lying on the floor. She was fully persuaded!

Abraham was another one who was fully persuaded, and he inherited the promise. He took the promise that was his and let the Light shine on the inside. He was not weak in faith any longer. He grew strong in faith. You can be the same way! It is your choice!

How much of God do you want? I want A L L that I can get. I am not satisfied. If you are satisfied, then you are backslidden! We must always want more. There is no such thing as standing still with God. You are either sliding forward or sliding back. God wants His best for you. You are precious in His sight. He sent His best for you. He loves you so much, but you must have a repentant heart to see this Gospel.

If you have not received Jesus Christ into your heart, pray this prayer:

Dear Heavenly Father, I come to you in the precious name of Jesus and by His blood shed for me. I repent of my sins and I accept you, Jesus, as my Lord and Savior. I believe that God raised Jesus from the dead and I confess Him right now as Lord of my life. Thank you, Jesus, for saving me. I am now your child.

In Jesus' name I pray, Amen.

WHICH FATHER ARE YOU FOLLOWING?

What you believe can bring victory or defeat in your life. Everybody believes in something. It is either the Truth or it is a lie. Be sure your light is not darkness. If it is a revelation from Heaven, it will produce Life. It is my desire that you will see through this message the TRUTH that God wants you to walk in victory. It is my desire to see the captives set free!

Jesus answered and said unto him, Verily, verily, I say unto thee, Except a man be born again, he cannot see the kingdom of God.

— John 3:3

Being born again, not of corruptible seed, but of incorruptible, by the word of God, which liveth and abideth forever.

— I Peter 1:23

But what saith it? The word is nigh thee, even in thy mouth, and in thy heart; that is, the word of faith, which we preach;

That if thou shalt confess with thy mouth the Lord Jesus, and shalt believe in thine heart that God hath raised him from the dead, thou shalt be saved.

For with the heart man believeth unto righteousness; and with the mouth confession is made unto salvation.

— Romans 10:8-10

CASSETTE TAPES by Robert Palmer

GLORY $4.00

Explains the Glory of God. Deals with God's
Glory manifest in His Church today. A message
for God's endtime army.

THE GOODNESS OF GOD $4.00

It is God's goodness that leads men to repentance. A vital message for those who want to
see their loved ones saved.

WHICH FATHER ARE YOU
FOLLOWING? $4.00

There are many voices in the world today.
This message deals with making the quality
decision to hear and follow God's voice.

SEEKING THE KINGDOM $4.00

The Kingdom of God is a reality. A message
of God's Kingdom established in the earth
today.

WALKING IN RIGHTEOUSNESS . . $4.00

In order to walk in the fulness of God's
blessings, the Church must understand her
position in Christ. This message will establish
the believer in God's Righteousness.

THE NAME OF JESUS $4.00

Our authority in the mighty name of Jesus
will come alive as you listen to this message.

GOODNESS AND MERCY $4.00

Reveals the character of God. This tape will
acquaint you with your Heavenly Father.